# A Myth in Reverse

# A Myth in Reverse

Selected Poems

by

Daphne Solá

© 2024 Daphne Solá. All rights reserved.
This material may not be reproduced in any form, published,
reprinted, recorded, performed, broadcast,
rewritten or redistributed without
the explicit permission of Daphne Solá.
All such actions are strictly prohibited by law.

Cover design by Shay Culligan
Cover image and author photo by Don Solá

ISBN: 978-1-63980-501-3

Kelsay Books
502 South 1040 East, A-119
American Fork, Utah 84003
Kelsaybooks.com

*This book is dedicated to Don Solá,
the first poet in my life,
and to our daughters and son,
granddaughters and grandsons,
each following his gifts
in their own way.*

# Acknowledgments

Thank you to the following publications, in which versions of these poems previously appeared:

*The Avocet (Winter 2022–23):* "In the Woods"

*The Avocet (Spring 2023):* "After a Hard Winter"

*Bluff & Vine Issue 6 (Fall 2022):* "I Learned Many Things from My Father"

*From The Finger Lakes: A Poetry Anthology (2016):* "We Are So Small"

*From the Finger Lakes: A Memoir Anthology (2021):* "Sixteen-Year-Old Usherette in a NY Theater"

# Contents

SECTION I: *OVERTURE*

| | |
|---|---|
| A Myth in Reverse | 17 |
| Looking Back | 19 |
| In the Pit of Consciousness | 21 |
| Poem in 10 Lines | 22 |
| Solfeggio | 23 |
| Grateful for Small Favors | 24 |
| Lagrimas Ultimas | 26 |
| July Twenty-Ninth | 28 |
| A Fateful Move | 29 |
| 10 Minutes and a Quarter-Turn | 30 |
| Sketch Book | 31 |
| It Is Time | 33 |

SECTION II: *FUGUE*

| | |
|---|---|
| When Papers Lie Like Fallen Leaves | 37 |
| The 'L' in Language | 39 |
| The Beekeeper | 40 |
| A Gift for My Father | 41 |
| Lollipop World | 42 |
| Schooling | 43 |
| Before School . . . | 44 |
| In the Deeps | 46 |

SECTION III: *BOLERO*

| | |
|---|---|
| Rage and Panes | 51 |
| From a Pillar of the Porch | 52 |
| Images | 53 |
| Pastorale | 54 |

Taking Flight　　　　　　　　　　　　　　　　55
Spring Equinox　　　　　　　　　　　　　　　57
In the Dark of Early Morning . . .　　　　　　58
The Brief Love of Earth and Moon　　　　　59
Wants and Waving Grasses　　　　　　　　　60
When the Grass Sighs　　　　　　　　　　　　62
What Happens, Happens　　　　　　　　　　63
Cat Fancies　　　　　　　　　　　　　　　　　64
Viento Malcriado　　　　　　　　　　　　　　65
Walking the Desert　　　　　　　　　　　　　66
Bittersweet　　　　　　　　　　　　　　　　　68
Your Loss Is a Bell . . .　　　　　　　　　　　69

## SECTION IV: *RALLENTANDO*

Journey　　　　　　　　　　　　　　　　　　73
Rights of Refusal　　　　　　　　　　　　　　75
Mourning Does Not Become Us　　　　　　77
Now . . .　　　　　　　　　　　　　　　　　　78
Social Distancing . . .　　　　　　　　　　　　79
In Lonely Times . . .　　　　　　　　　　　　81

## SECTION V: *ARIAS*

Absence　　　　　　　　　　　　　　　　　　85
Waiting　　　　　　　　　　　　　　　　　　　86
Pensamiento　　　　　　　　　　　　　　　　87
A World Turned Half-Around　　　　　　　88
Las Manos　　　　　　　　　　　　　　　　　89
Lu You's Passion　　　　　　　　　　　　　　90
Reluctant Nymph　　　　　　　　　　　　　91
An Apiary Tale　　　　　　　　　　　　　　　92

## SECTION VI: *AMOROSO*

| | |
|---|---|
| Ojime Bead | 97 |
| On a Slow Burn | 98 |
| On an Irish Hillside | 99 |
| Trying to Speak in a World Full of Strangers | 100 |
| When I Passed Your Chair | 102 |
| Frisson | 103 |
| Beached | 104 |
| Song of the Blood | 105 |
| The Taste of Sweetness | 106 |
| Twenty Times a Day | 107 |
| Poem for Next Tuesday | 108 |
| On Not Being Lysistrata | 109 |
| The Reality of Flesh | 110 |
| To My Surprise | 111 |
| Through a Mist Darkly | 112 |
| On Fait de la Comédie | 113 |

## SECTION VII: *CAPRICCIO*

| | |
|---|---|
| Of Dregs and Legs | 117 |
| The Gates of Heaven | 118 |
| The Trouble with Venerable Maxims . . . | 120 |

## SECTION VIII: *SONATA*

| | |
|---|---|
| Beginnings | 125 |
| Shoo, Shoo, Babies, | 126 |
| Memoir of a Five-Year-Old | 128 |
| In a New Place | 129 |
| Children's Rhymes | 130 |

| | |
|---|---|
| Some Kids Have It Easy . . . | 132 |
| My Hour at the Museum | 134 |
| Going to the Movies | 135 |
| Memories of New York, a Nickel's Worth | 137 |
| Ode to a Diamond Ring | 139 |
| Quién Era? | 140 |
| Other Rooms, Other Realities | 142 |
| A Beautiful Being | 144 |
| It Is Ignoble . . . | 146 |
| Idiots and Savants in the Labor Room | 147 |
| October Birthday | 149 |
| Continuity | 151 |
| Goodbye, Sweet Gallery | 153 |
| I Want the Sun to Burn Me | 155 |
| We Are So Small | 156 |

# SECTION I: *OVERTURE*

A Myth in Reverse
Looking Back
In the Pit of Consciousness
Poem in 10 Lines
Solfeggio
Grateful for Small Favors
Lagrimas Ultimas
July Twenty-Ninth
A Fateful Move
10 Minutes and a Quarter-Turn
Sketch Book
It Is Time

# A Myth in Reverse

*of Daphne and Apollo*

If you come with me
we will follow a path
covered with red leaves the color of autumn,
or possibly with the blood of animals
who only a few hours ago
came this way, howled
and fought to the death.

We will build a house here,
or climb trees
and throw ourselves down
on a wide branch where the wind
caresses our limbs and, finally,
we sleep.

We spend our days reading books
with covers made of bark
and pages within of parchment,
we eat the abundant fruits,
but avoid the nuts
a passing whimsy in taste.

We do not fear the serpents
that inhabit this forest
for they are busy elsewhere
and when we bite into the apples
no one comes to punish us
because we are not in the Garden of Eden,
we are living a Greek myth
in reverse,
where Daphne does not save herself
in the watery embrace of her father,

she invites her destiny,
to be a nymph, pursued
and captured
by Apollo.

October 2012

# Looking Back

When my father said,
I'm going to knock the stuffing out of you
we knew to recoil
and try to save ourselves.
He was not given to thinking
in euphemisms,
like a good Victorian father
he was quite capable
of boxing our ears
which is not really
as benign as it sounds.

All that is long past
but when cutting words
knock the stuffing out of us
we know to recoil,
to try and save ourselves
we curl around the pain
an instinct learned and not forgotten.
If there is a wildly beating pulse
we have an outer self unmarked
and leave it so
the means of getting through today
and all the days and nights to come.

We find some solace in remembering
that the hands that boxed our ears
also cut and ground,
filed and glued,
so that his Victorian daughters
did not lack for perfect toys.

My father had few words for us,
all he gave was in his hands.
He did not talk
we did not cry,
perhaps without knowing it at the time
our fearful skin and our perfect toys
formed a silent bond
among us.

March 2010

# In the Pit of Consciousness

In the pit of consciousness,
questions root about and nudge at us
like blind newborns.
Why did fish climb out of the water
on rudimentary stumps,
what hubris made man decide
he could rocket to the moon?

Try putting out your finger and touching
*urge* or *need,*
admit to letting love and non-love
jerk us about,
then try to transform *grief* and *rapture*
into a mathematical equation.

It's a balm to return
to a world
offering comfort in the tangible,
and in isolated moments
in a very real room
we can listen to music
where the sublime emerges
from a diatonic scale,
and, standing in the kitchen,
we handily distinguish
bouillabaisse
from a bowl of porridge.

August 2012

# Poem in 10 Lines

In these days, so bitter, so ugly,
I present to you ten seconds of a softer time,
     with a long curve like the equator,
     like the neck of a swan.
If you have pain, I offer the pressure of my arms
     encircling you like the equator.
And if you suffer because nothing lasts,
    I have for you, a kiss,
      a moment sweet and stretched
like the neck of a swan.

October 2018

# Solfeggio

We used to play in a soft key,
a round key . . .
A flat major . . . sol, la, ti, do
*la* for *lust,*
two bodies, four hands,
applied with great finesse
when a shift to F sharp major,
brought new brilliance to our playing,
and *la* transformed itself
to *ti* for tenderness.

Solfeggio ties us to the music,
notes that dance before our eyes
above the staff
below the staff
half notes, whole notes
all aligned.
Do I see a simple key change?
no, I think it is a sea change
impressed upon our keyboard
where black speaks out for body
and white shuts out the mind.

December 2012

# Grateful for Small Favors

For two days
I had a terrible pain in my foot
I could not walk
or put my foot on the ground
I could not drag on a boot.

See then, I am not a hapless king
suffering in a renaissance palace, I live
in the rocket-to-the-moon twenty-first century
and was given a medication
which, true to its promise,
sent the pain away,

but behind the promise
lay threats called side effects,
I might have thinning blood
suffer heart or liver damage
headache
nausea
insomnia
depression
an attack of hyper-activity
or dizziness

I would slip on the ice
squint in bright sunlight
shudder in the rain
and I would lose all my best friends.
I searched the small print carefully
and looked for the worst threat of all . . .
which was not there.

It did not say
You may not write a poem!

So I have written a poem.

January 2019

# Lagrimas Ultimas

*Last Tears*

The last time I cried was the evening
my husband died.
In the weeks and months before,
rigid with containment
we were living outside ourselves
in the dry air that surrounded him,
his breaths were our breaths
as we watched his struggles
with a body that would not die.

The intensity of our absorption
was useless, even self-indulgent,
and in lucid moments
he wickedly brought us out of it,
'Next time you bring dinner,' he said,
'make it a good bottle of wine,
none of that New York stuff.' and,
looking out the window,
'Am I going to be in this bed
for the rest of my life?'

In the darkening room
on that final evening
we all sat silent
crying a river of tears
which carried us along with a force
that returned us to ourselves,
fluidity being restored
to our dry mouths
and aching limbs.

The children would go on to swim
in whatever turbulent waters
they encountered,
but I saw myself,
at least at that time,
cast up on a bank, grieving anew,
because in a solitary act of possession
my husband had taken with him
my last tears.

August 2008

# July Twenty-Ninth

This is the day he died
a tug at my core
but with the passing of time
there is less to say.

It is our good fortune that
some things
are ineradicable
his laugh
his beautiful hair
his unfathomable kindness.

February 2018

# A Fateful Move

Take a New York girl
and transport her to the country where
every day is a discovery
Nature is not confined to a city park
but stretches outside the door
to fields and woods beyond.
Spring could not be more miracled
than in her eye.

Winter has the dress of snow on
every twig and branch
March is a trial, grass still brown
between muddy patches.
Then comes the sound
of peepers that drench the evening air
birdsong greeting the morning sun
foretells warmth and the burst
of close-held buds.

But nothing can top the arrival in May
of the great blue heron
sighted in his one-legged stance,
immobile, at the edge of the pond
hidden mayhem
in his long neck
his rapier beak.

In a changing world
who would wish this all away
at best, with thoughtlessness
at worst,
with purposeful consumption.

April 2019

# 10 Minutes and a Quarter-Turn

I am spurred to write, if only to explain to myself,
    how it happened that I had on my back
    in bold red outline
the full imprint of my husband's hand.
The ties between us were so strong, we could
    pull and tug,
    strain and weave
and still remain fast friends and lovers.

And so . . . the friendly wrestling match,
    two antagonists who fought
like pugilists with ungloved hands,
until, in an unguarded moment
    twisting about with too much speed
his hand hit my back with enough force
    to leave on my skin an image of his palm
    and every one of his fingers.

The effect was unknown until the following morning
when I sat on a modeling stand for a college art class,
    all innocent nakedness.
Surely they had seen nude models before?
But, when every ten minutes the stand was given
    a quarter turn,
I was left . . . the professor was maintaining
    a bemused silence . . .
and I was left to contemplate an expression
    of astonishment and curiosity
    on every student face.

September 2018

# Sketch Book

*For Don's birthday*

When I put pen to paper
you were captured
painting the ceiling,
at a café in Spain,
hanging diapers,
gripping a pipe with your teeth,
and a favorite drawing
that shattered the paper
with your laughter.

There are so many places that
bear your imprint.
Now that you are no longer here
I look to the painted doorjamb
the worn old captain's chair
in your office,
the tire tracks of the Subaru that
took you away and brought you home,
a bundle of bent-eared airline tickets
and those letters from India
which were your first imploring words
to me
buried in descriptions of a strange
new place
and a war.

But I heard you
and waited for you
and now on the other side of the dream
I have one hundred
two hundred
three hundred drawings
each tearing off a bit of your presence
and transforming them,

it's what black ink on white paper can do
but, like so many tactile things
it is not enough
it is not enough.

June 2010

# It Is Time

Wear a mask! they say,
when it is time to find a cloak
that shields from head to foot.

Stay away! they say
this is not the time
to meet and clasp lover or friend.

Do not breathe! they say,
when, at any time,
breath is life.

In a chivying tone, Are you lonely?
Are you complaining? Then it is time
to raise your eyes,

Start listening, turn to face the rain
and drink the wetness
though it drenches,

Walk on floating lily pads where
placing your feet is a gamble,
try not to sink and drown.

Bring to mind all the things that fly,
birds, kites,
dandelion puffs,

Revel in them, and perhaps
the vines that bind your feet
will give way

And you will tread easily on clouds
for a single hour

with luck, for a single day.

July 2020

# SECTION II: *FUGUE*

### POETRY

When Papers Lie Like Fallen Leaves
The 'L' in Language

### MEMORIES OF CHILDHOOD

The Beekeeper
A Gift for My Father
Lollipop World
Schooling
Before School . . .
In the Deeps

# When Papers Lie Like Fallen Leaves

When papers lie like fallen leaves,
some floating lightly down
others beaten into submission
as pulp is beaten in the making
of a single sheet,
the poet stands above them,
a Dalíesque figure
with aching jaws
and a long tongue.

Not a pretty picture
and strangely at odds
with his presenting
to an unwilling public
delicately flared nostrils
and flowing locks
carefully deposed about his head
to diffuse the knowledge
that he is a pugilist.

Back at his desk, poetry is a fight
a whittling down,
and the skeleton that remains
has the earmarks
of leanness and durability.
Some among us
embrace its Giacometti attenuation,
knowing how easy it is
to taunt with excess
and beguile with soft textures.
We beg the poet to be indomitable,
to gather up

those white sheets of paper
and fill the pages for us
with the hard, the metaphoric,
even the indecipherable.

April 2014

# The 'L' in Language

*A short journey in the English language*
takes us to clustered consonants
portraying angst and crippling,
*trudge* and *crutch*
*wrench* and *fraught,*

but the word I cannot bear to contemplate
is *anguish*. It has an upward arc,
the bell of *ang,* then a wrenching turn
in midair as it drops
to the crushing sound of grief.

To be in a state of anguish is to have the word
ringing in your ears,
somehow blinding the eyes
and cruelly blanking out
all other sounds

of life and living.

March 2012

# The Beekeeper

My father loved bees and
it was the one thing I loved about him.
He moved among them
pulling out trays, brushing them off his sleeves
and always holding a gravelly conversation with them.
He was shrouded in netting—but carelessly—
all his trust in the close relationship
he had with his charges
and the bees never disappointed,
they only stung the neighbors.

Away from his bees and roses
my father was a fierce man,
burly, gruff and at the least displeasure
quite capable of striking
his wife and two daughters.
The elder girl left home when she was eighteen
suffused with an anger that never abated
and a few years later I followed,
but I could not bear that my father
would never see either one of us again
so I visited from time to time.

Though we knew the worth of those visits
I remember cool, tenuous relations
with me trying to quell my fearful skin,
but it grew easier over the years
because I knew
each time I took my leave,
when my mother's back was turned,
my father would thrust into my hand
a jar of honey for my long-absent sister,
"Och, take this," he would say,
"I know she will be wanting it."

January 2011

# A Gift for My Father

For his birthday,
I made him a shirt,
cut and sewn by hand,

every stitch.

With such evidence of effort
I wish it had more closely resembled
a shirt bought in a store,

it did not,

but when he wore it
he smiled and I could see
the bruises behind his eyes

almost disappear.

For my birthday
my father made for me a lamp
fashioned from a ballet figurine

with a silken shade.

I didn't really care
for its china-doll look
but ever afterwards

he could turn aside

our frequent bouts of anger
by saying,
'Do you remember,

I gave you a lamp?'

February 2012

# Lollipop World

I want to remember a time
when no one had died,
a lollipop existence
still in its wrapper.

Just after the sticky paper
came off
was the promise of
lemon, grape or cherry, and

I barely noticed the fraud
in every lick or
the awful flavor
because as yet

no one had died.

November 2011

# Schooling

When blows fall
and you are too small
to fight back
one thing you can do
is cower
sometimes weeping
more often not.
You listen to the hissing words
*I'll teach you a lesson you won't forget!*
and hear them
turn upon themselves
because the lesson learned
while parrying blows
is that you can
and will
survive.

February 2011

# Before School . . .

*(A lullaby)*

Before school brings me into focus
I sit on the edge of the bed
dangling my legs

my toes do not reach the floor
that's how I know
I am still small

I sing to myself, my voice
high and clear
but outside

the voices rasp and break
some in laughter
some in anger

their words fly out
and hit the wall
I do not want to join them

I stop swinging my legs
make my singing secret
curl my fingers tightly

round the soft rag arm
of my favorite doll
that's how I know

I am still small
she . . . there are no boy dolls . . .
has a song for me,

close your eyes
close your ears,

tuck your head into a pillow

at least for tonight,
I promise,
to keep tomorrow's sounds

from coming through your door.

August 2020

# In the Deeps

The child stands
at the bottom of the sea
where everything is easy
one kick
and he will shoot off
bank smoothly
turn a somersault
and float to a soft landing.

All around him
are so many things to play with,
fish and ferns
and, best of all, little monsters
who tease and sting without mercy.
When the child runs
he knows his legs can stretch a mile
and appears water-impeded
and slow-motion
only in the eyes
of the shore-bound watchers.

Layers and layers of water
protect him
from what blurrily lies above.
Up there, air
(what *is* that?)
winds about silently,
unseen and unsupportive.

The land creatures
have eyes that watch
but do not see,

they cannot bound in liquid leaps
push pearls from their noses
cozy up
to sleeping barracudas
grip baby eels between their toes.

The child stands
at the bottom of the sea
then lies back, arms stretched out
legs dangling,
swept in to a current that,
like a rip-tide, will carry him
willy-nilly upward and out
through all the protective layers,
until finally released
he crawls out
on the gritty sand
and must learn to breathe and walk
in the dry
and unforgiving air.

May 2018

# SECTION III: *BOLERO*

## NATURE AND DON SOLÁ

Rage and Panes
From a Pillar of the Porch
Images
Pastorale
Taking Flight
Spring Equinox
In the Dark of Early Morning . . .
The Brief Love of Earth and Moon
Wants and Waving Grasses
When the Grass Sighs
What Happens, Happens
Cat Fancies
Viento Malcriado
Walking the Desert
Bittersweet
Your Loss Is a Bell . . .

# Rage and Panes

It's hard to see out a window
which is clouded by rain
and futile to look into
the window of memory
where rain falls
in thick droplets
obscuring vision.

Memory could be,
as in an old house,
fashioned into six or
twelve-light windows that
randomly fracture each image,
but the flooded pane
with a large crack across it
is rage
suppressed, of course,
because a child is not allowed rage.

Perhaps better to turn away
and brush the rain
clinging to my eyelashes.
In my house, there are six
and twelve-light panes
bringing warmth and radiance
into the present
and the hope
that my children's rage . . .
in whatever pocket of their lives . . .
is paled by the steely love
we all have for each other.

November 2020

# From a Pillar of the Porch

I am singing back to the robin . . .
how bumptious can you be? . . .
who is building a nest on a pillar of the porch,
persistent, defiant, ready to fly out
        and chivy the mortals who disturb her.

She is making a terrible mess at the foot of the pillar
which I humbly clean up every morning,
        stray bits of broken grass
        rejects from the pliable spears
        that will make her home.
she'll have none of it, my ministrations,
and it is enviable how sure my robin-mother is
        of what she has to do,
disturbance and abandon are not in her vocabulary.

Sing back to me, red robin,
woven into your nest are the threads of implacable need,
I await the first faint cheeps, pulses of life
that are your triumph,
they will gladden me
and brighten my day.

May 2019

# Images

The pretty shadows
On my window are only
A visitation
Both ephemeral and fixed
When the earth moves
They will not be seen again
Until next year.

February 2010

## Pastorale

At the edge of a meadow
stand three sisters
so close together
they climb past each other
to reach their patch of sky.

With their inner arms they caress each other
a corporal linking of shortened boughs
meeting a sister's shortened boughs
needle fans brushing needle fans
their outer arms long and free
to dip and cut the air
until the swaying begins
when just a puff of wind can move them,
not very far, but enough
to define them as three white pines
seeds sown by an unknowing foot,
a cavorting squirrel
a ferreting mouse.

The three sisters are so young,
with a terrible hunger for light
and an aspiration to tallness
beyond the tops of familial evergreens,
if innocent in their longings
they are also foolhardy,
a bolt of lightning, if it comes,
will strike, not one,
but all three
the meadow will burn
and the landscape they now grace
will be changed forever.

June 2013

# Taking Flight

*A March Poem*


Winter revels in its icy grip,
        pulling back in early March
then roaring forward,
        just to make us squeal.
But winter's defeat is in the air when
        we hear the silly ducks
and we greet them
        with a mix of derision and joy.

They make us laugh as they wheel, circle and
        finally drop down
        to our small pond
Too many, too many!
No room, no room!
And the latecomers stand, looking nonplussed
        and foolish
        on the edge of the ice-pan
still covering half the rippling water.

It is such a comfort to know that foolish
        also belongs to the animal world.
Before we see the panorama
        we hear the squawking
and assume the ducks are spring-intoxicated
        as are we.
Even with the pond vastly over-crowded,
        they quack to their brethren
        flying over,

'Come down! Come down!'
and here they come, until the ice and water
        are black with their feathery bodies.
What we count on is their appearance
        each spring, inspiration for us

to include un-flappable determination
       in our own lives,
our toes gripping the edge of an ice-pan,
       ready to plunge into cold waters,

       And soon, like the silly March ducks,
       we will have wings and foolishness
           to give us flight
             from old domains
into a crowded and verdant world.

March 2019

# Spring Equinox

Sun touches my window
And the pond ripples across my ceiling
Water transformed into light.

March 2010

# In the Dark of Early Morning . . .

a long white cloud lies on the chill waters of the lake
      a deep lake
      a miles-long lake
that centers my life.

If I travel east, north or south
      the lake and its wooded hills
      fill the horizon
the water is not blue,
      not azure
      often a slate-to-silver gray.
Longevity is the language that it speaks
      the lapping and
      running white-caps
it's singing voice.

On a dull winter day, pulling no light
      from the sky
      and with the south inlet icing up
the lake's cold sheen looks
      like permanence,
but on the day when temperatures rise
the white cloud that rests,
      opaque and heavy
      along its surface
lifts, and frees itself like a living body,
      each wisp an arm or a leg
disappearing into the warm daylight
      above the lake.

Perhaps telling us that
      not all beautiful things
      are meant to last.

November 2021

# The Brief Love of Earth and Moon

At the rising of Moon,
her cold round face
is warmly tinged, elliptical
and shimmering around the edges.
Magnetized,
she wills herself
to stay . . .
a giant hands-breadth
from Earth.

Tides surge landward,
pulled by Moon
in the struggle
to enmesh herself
but her grip loosens . . . now
no more than a stag-leap
from Earth.

When night winds subside,
attraction dims and
Moon loses her shimmering edge . . .
and her will
to linger.

No longer clinging
to darkened tree limbs and shadowed fields
she turns a cold round face
to Earth,
and pulling free,
begins her climb
up and across
an infinity of sky.

June 2011

# Wants and Waving Grasses

In the early morning
we wanted a pond
and wished away the marshy ground
where flowing water
was trapped
by rampant grasses
that themselves wished to be a dream
       of thin foliage and pendant flowers.

Soon the morning mist began to rise
       and our wish became so strong
we welcomed a bulldozer
       the man in a peaked hat
who shoveled his way through the
       tangled mass
and spread on waiting banks
       mangled grass
          to fade and die.

In the heat of day,
the pond came into being
the stirred mud sank
       and the water was so clear
I could see my hand
       submerged in it.

But the day grows long
we have what we wanted
and as evening shadows lengthen
I want to slow their descent.
The pond, once so transparent,
       is showing its age.

There is no way to wish away the silt
    that creeps steadily down
      a farm-cropped hill
or the islands of green that rise up
    like continents.

It's been a day and years-long struggle to
    keep relentless change at bay
but struggle has its own rewards
    and, in the end,
we would not want it
    any other way.

July 2020

# When the Grass Sighs

Pond, do you hear Grass sighing?
The rasp of blades is sharp
eager to bend and sway . . .
or to be bent
by foot or knee or hands . . .
but in just a little time
each bent blade
lifts a seeded head
to link once more with Wind.

Pond, you must listen to Wind
sighing out a warning,
about to cast off
his tempered mien.
He wants to rough himself
against your shining skin,
send ripples of discontent
across your stillness
and break the mirror image
into jagged shards.

Do you hear them,
do you see them, Pond?
They hover on your bank,
passion turned
to tease and torment.
Tables turned,
now Wind and Grass
gaze upon their own reflections,
trapped and trembling,
drowning slowly
in your depths.

May 2022

# What Happens, Happens

An un-choreographed movement of my foot
sends a stone skittering sideways
a low arc, a click, a whoosh
and it shoots into icy water.

In the rustling grasses that grace the edge of the pond
a fox creeps, his nose leading him to Lily, the white duck
and when he seizes her by the neck
her wintry death does not disturb the water.

Calm settles on the perimeter of the pond
only George, mate to Lily, suffers her loss,
no quack equal to his pain, he looks to save himself,
slips down the grassy bank on his feathery bottom

and paddles away in the rippling, healing water.

What happens, happens.

May 2019

# Cat Fancies

I love cats,
so sure of themselves,
muscles running like ropes
under the skin
claws strong enough to grip
and paws powerful enough to bruise
when a casual swipe leaves its mark.

"I am here!" says my cat, "and you
passed me by without notice!
If you turn back in surprise
you will feel my gold-green eyes
boring holes
in your inadequate body.

Can you leap up many times
your own length?
Can you crouch in the grass
quivering with the energy
to spring on hapless prey?"

I am humbled and
with cat-like mien
I slink off
to open a can
of his favorite food

"It is all too much," he says, in my wake,
"I'll leave off chivying to savor sleep."
but I notice he keeps one slitted eye
half-open
to take in all of the world
he cares to see.

November 2016

# Viento Malcriado

(*Wicked Wind*)

Wind does not care
for predictability
preferring to bend grasses left
then right
to rough rusty windmills
into creaky motion
and spiral under leeward doors.

Listen to what the wind is saying
who can tell if I'll prevail?
Who can tell me how to blow?
You have to take me as I am
wayward
rebellious
the last free spirit.

September 2011

# Walking the Desert


We were new to Polacca, a pueblo
        ninety miles east of Grand Canyon,
but we tried to wear our eastern naïveté lightly.
It was our luck that the Tewa were living
        on top of the mesa
        in their summer quarters
and could lend us a winter house
        on the vast plain below.
We could stand in front of our new abode
and see distances heretofore unimagined.

With pen and ink, I made drawing after drawing
        of sand and mesquite
        and far-off mountains in black-and-white.
What I could not expect was that one day
        the black horizon would become
        a slow-moving cloud,
threatening, because it was walking towards us
        across the desert
and could be seen for hours before
        the wind and rain came upon us.
Many years later the desert is drier and the Rain Dance
        of the Tewas becomes more desperate.

We had learned how violent happenings
        in the Southwest have their own pace,
a pace now embodied by drought after drought.
I remember with some pain, that my inky drawings
        could be made and finished
before the first blotting raindrops
        splashed down

and I would watch as the black cloud
       passed us,
and resumed its slow walk  across
         an endless stretch of desert sand.

March 2019

## Bittersweet

The summer that my husband died
I seemed to move,
through a cloud of friends
all asking, "What can I do?"
and the answer was, "Nothing."

But my children took hold
of the cipher I had become,
they functioned for me—
visiting banks and lawyers
clerks and directors—
and claimed that about every three hours
I would stand in front of them
and say,
"What do I do now?"

It was a surreal world
that slips and slides in memory
and does not hold still
to be recorded.
But what I remember best
is that those children pruned trees and
raked leaves,
and when Michèle went out and
bought a basket of peaches,
at the end of the day
we had pots of homemade jam
illuminating the kitchen windowsill.

March 29, 2010

## Your Loss Is a Bell . . .

ringing out over a pond which sustained
        our love for natural things
and now sustains my ravaged memory
        of grassy banks,
        an old house
        and older trees
that bend over a gravel drive
        leading to a kitchen door
        that scrapes against a stony porch
as if to impede our entry into
        a place we lived in and loved
        for so many years.

There were twelve-light windows, some cracked
        and some with whorls of light
        to prove their hand-blown origin.
The bell rings out and will not be stilled
even for the squabbling ducks, the heron
        standing on one leg
        in rippling water
among a myriad of darting dragonflies.

I grasp at all of these things
        but the bell of your loss rings for me
because I cannot find you anywhere.

February 2020

# SECTION IV: *RALLENTANDO*

MOURNING, PANDEMIC, ISOLATION

Journey
Rights of Refusal
Mourning Does Not Become Us
Now . . .
Social Distancing . . .
In Lonely Times . . .

# Journey

The path leads steeply up the hill
and appears to end
      at the horizon.
More fools, we,
to believe in that hard line
      against the sky.
It defies definition
moving as we move
      in a slow dance
      back     and back
now flattened grass
now forest
another step and it becomes a mirage
      of transparent water
shimmering below the clouds.

And if we cannot tear our eyes away
      to look at the path
        under our feet
it will be our fate
      to miss the sand
      and the stones,
arranged with a sense of the diabolical
      to make us stumble.

How do we train our eyes
      to follow
        these chameleon changes
when even a sidelong glance will delay us
      in our climb?
In time, we learn to distinguish
      north and south
      above and below
      good and evil

but it is a long art,
        an arduous art,
the journey from child to man.

# Rights of Refusal

I walk to the edge of a cliff
and measure the drop
to the bottom
but halfway down, I see a clump of
bushes, clinging,
but spiky enough to catch
and rough me up,
then toss me to the wind
as not worth keeping.

By hesitating, I had gained time
and returning to my house
I see a bee is angrily
climbing the kitchen window.
I could crush it
the sting is there, after all,
at-the-ready.
but I resist mayhem,
take a dishtowel
enfold his buzzy little self
and at the open door
I let him go,

Looking back,
engaged in reckoning,
I had found no comfort
in stepping off the edge,
killing a bee,
or in my withdrawal
from either of these fateful moves.
The only thing I achieved
was the right of refusal,

but I know that when the last day comes . . .
implacable . . .
yielding no rights . . .
I will be afraid.

May 2018

# Mourning Does Not Become Us

Whatever threatens to upend us
I will not trade on impending gloom . . .
ill health abroad
the doubling and tripling of hurricanes
the littered agony of oceans . . .
all woes too easy to mourn
when living was never meant to be easy
neither labor, nor creative art
nor peaceful sleep.

What use to mourn,
our hands wrung into uselessness?
Better to shake our heads free
of flying objects
that batter our ears and
blind our eyes
take mourn and drown it
in the nearest lagoon.

If I have never believed in panaceas
there is such a thing
as linked arms in friendship,
and prayer made potent
for devout and skeptic alike.
If we are a resilient breed
it's time to buckle ingenious weapons
to our belts
and create morning
out of a setting sun.

November 2020

# Now . . .

living in a time
of impoverishment
denied people
therefore the feel of skin
therefore love
we are left only with things
mute and immutable.
But we will find a way out
with a libido of the mind
spinning words
from the nib of a pen . . .
to paper, and
into another's hand.
And when a return page
comes back to us
what we hold in our hand
is quick to the senses . . .
things come alive again
bodies a palpable presence
and as time passes
we will hardly remember
excoriating emptiness.

February 2021

# Social Distancing . . .

has denied me you
which is supposed to save my life
a worthy cause
but happens to enclose an agony.

I decide I need a cup of coffee
I am so bored with
my tea-drinking self

and it reminds me of the dark black stuff
you drink, the making of which
you explain to me

every morning I wake up in your house,
a repetition, one of many repetitions sprinkled
on our lives . . . like sugar.

I have a cat, and our independent lives
are full of such gritty sweetness.
When we cuddle together,

not you and me, I was thinking of
my cat,
he extends a paw, no claw,

and touches my chin, a display
of affection, atypical
of his kind,

he is . . .
you are . . .
demanding, quixotic, endearing.

I have lost my cat and express my rage
at this act of fate by being angry at things,
the dish I dropped and broke,

the pulled curtain that crashed down,
the donned coat whose other sleeve
I cannot find with a flailing hand.

Perhaps I will get another cat
but what can I do
now faced with the loss

of a visible irreplaceable you.

April 2020

# In Lonely Times . . .

I pluck at the golden threads
that weave themselves
into the mottled fabric of my life

lighting the humdrum
and turning it into a garment that prickles
next to my skin, but when I put it on

I become the squirrel scampering at full speed
across frozen ground
intent on some important errand.

I sleep like my fulvous cat, who,
with slow breath and his tail curled round,
makes a warm and perfect circle,

and if I dream of effortless flight, I know enough
to savor a return to earth and
its tawny friendships.

I reach out an arm to touch one of those friends,
and in a proud yet humble voice,
I say

*'You are a goldmine of provocative thought!*
*Oh, dear friend,*
*Don't go anywhere soon*
*In these lonely times*
*I need you.'*

March 2021

# SECTION V: *ARIAS*

## EMOTIONS

Absence
Waiting
Pensamiento
A World Turned Half-Around
Las Manos
Lu You's Passion
Reluctant Nymph
An Apiary Tale

# Absence

Although endless tasks
tumble over themselves
to fill my days
there is intrusion on my thoughts
little stabs of memory
of what we say
and what we do
that tear the fabric of my life,
the fragile cloth
that offered taut resistance
now is loosened
and through the rents
come tiny waves
of simple longing
just to hear your voice.

March 2010

# Waiting

Waiting is a woman's game
Unwilling self, I'll learn it
And submit to hearing footfalls
Where there are none.

January 2010

# Pensamiento

It's people
Who have not lived
Through fearsome times
Who make the harshest judgments

March 2010

# A World Turned Half-Around

I allowed myself to love you
big mistake
a world turns upside-down
and saints no longer
walk on water.
To believe in saints?
another big mistake
to believe is to trust.

See love standing firm
on two legs
but when one of them breaks
trust can only stumble
and fall

I want to see you, feel you,
throw myself at you
on you
or at least on your mercy
hopeless
mercy does not live
in the same house
as hubris.

My eyes close
but belief dangles,
trying to hold on,
and I dare not look back
to where I allowed myself
to love you.

February 2013

## Las Manos

If you were to go away
I don't know about the rest of you
but it's the hands
that I would miss
and ache for.

In Spanish
with a curious commingling
of masculine and feminine endings
*las manos* are never marked
as *your* hands
or *my* hands
it is always *the* hands
and the syntax of that foreign tongue
somehow, at a discreet distance,
takes care of identifying
whose hands they are.

I've buried that alien syntax
somewhere inside of me
with no accompanying image
but the tactile sense of your hands
is fixed and deep
*las manos* with that distant marker
rising to the surface
only when I think
what it would be
to lose you.

March 2010

## Lu You's Passion

In a fit of passion, Lu You
wrote a poem on a wall.
With this wild gesture
he begged forgiveness from a lost love—
his wife, scorned in his house
and chilled by a harsh wind,
the mother of Lu You.

Too late, the lady left, but
in her turn scribed these words,
'I swallow my tears and wear a smile,
a thin façade that hides my anguish,
I ask one thing,
do not forget me,'
in fading voice,
'do not forget me.'

The poem, lifting off the wall,
hovers in mid-air
and in that current
flows down to us
centuries obliterated,

And in this time, when we claim
a new-found love
no less intense than the master poet's,
we craft words that fly between us
with no thought of pain or chilling harshness
and yet reserve a knowing space that,
should the need arise,
will tell us where to find a wall.

February 2011

# Reluctant Nymph

Make me shout

I want to sleep

Pull me forward

I want to lie down
in silence and pull leaves
over my eyes

Make me cry out and rough
light and shadow across my arms
until they burn

Resistance lasts only so long

I can feel it coming
and know what
has to be done

I will press my palm
hard
into a patch of sun.

November 2011

# An Apiary Tale

When I need to sleep
I ask you to tell me again
the story of
how wonderful you are
and drowsily I answer back
with the story of
how wonderful I am.

Settling into familiar warmth
each of us starts out
with the tale of two bees
flying over a flower patch
who collide in midair
and fall to the ground,
two fuzzy bodies,
stunned, but live enough
to crawl towards each other
over the humpy earth,
me smelling of honey,
and you, producing a high buzz
with your intellectual antennae.

When we return, each
to his own hive,
we stop in the doorway
and twitch out legs
in a mad dance
eager to tell all the other bees
what can be found
in a sunny patch of flowers.

Then summer ends
and snow covers the meadow,
but before we drop
into wintry sleep

I ask you to tell me
a new story
of how delicious I am
and in a contented drone
I mumble back
the story
of how remarkable you are.

July 2016

# SECTION VI: *AMOROSO*

### EROTICA

Ojime Bead
On a Slow Burn
On an Irish Hillside
Trying to Speak in a World Full of Strangers
When I Passed Your Chair
Frisson
Beached
Song of the Blood
The Taste of Sweetness
Twenty Times a Day
Poem for Next Tuesday
On Not Being Lysistrata
The Reality of Flesh
To My Surprise
Through a Mist Darkly
On Fait de la Comédie

# Ojime Bead

I hold in my hand
a round ivory bead
an *ojime* carving of masks
with tiny eyes
and mouths with little agonies.

Hold still, ivory dancing ball
dizzy is a new word
in my vocabulary . . .
but it's not the sphere
that's spinning,

it's me . . . it's me . . .

that's what happiness does.

June 2012

# On a Slow Burn

It is not a single kiss that changes our lives
        but an abundance of them
Move down the body and talk
        about arms and hands
Lovers are not the ones who set the stage
        for carnal desire
Long before they appear
        babies are nuzzled and squeezed
Families gather and hug
        sister to brother
        cousin to cousin
Such benign friction
        even among friends.

Then let the lovers come swinging along
        each one unique, or in hungry droves
The body, furnished with all the moving parts
        will know what to do . . .
if it has been touched
        and touched again.

Down to the fingertips, skin must be pricked alive
        nerve endings brought to a slow burn
Sense and movement are like words and phrases
        in a language, once learned,
        not easily forgotten.

July 2017

## On an Irish Hillside

I know the wool that covers us
took a shearer
at least ten downward strokes

but once released
the sheep trotted off
naked

into spring air like cracked ice
and waited for the sun
to come up.

Like the sheep
I know a taut enfolding arm
and could lie naked

in spring grass
but I pull
the ten-stroke blanket up

and all night long
warm, enfolded,
I breathe air like cracked ice.

November 2011

# Trying to Speak in a World Full of Strangers

In a city full of strangers,
I say it with half-closed eyes,
*love on a long afternoon* . . .
but my words bound and rebound
from one stone tower to another,
then fall to the asphalt street,
and are ground to bits
by truck after car after truck.

In a hotel full of strangers,
with tight-shut eyes I say it again,
but the rays of the sun
coming through the blinds
burn my words into dust
that will be swept away in the morning
by a chambermaid who speaks to us
in an unknown language.

In this turbulent city,
I want to show you
a green park full of strangers,
a park with a Shakespeare Garden,
bronze statues of men with lifeless eyes,
and a fountain
where the young sit silhouetted
by rainbow'd water.

A fitting place for me to say it
over and over again,
but, the young are absorbed,
the stone statues are unmoved
and the long afternoon shadows
tell me it is late
and I must wait until we return home.

There, we are surrounded
by the doubling and tripling of a green park,
shale cliffs soft to the eye
and almost everyone knows us,
so I don't need to say a word
because, one look,
and even the strangers among us
take what I might say for granted.

May 2013

# When I Passed Your Chair

When I, wearing black
first stood in front of you
and you said, *I'm sorry to hear* . . .
I could believe you
but listening to other people use the same words
*I'm sorry to hear* . . .
they had no measure.
You I believed
because I saw the loss
still in your face.

We might never have been invited to that dinner
we did not even sit at the same table
it was all conversation with other people
and I did not speak a word to you
until, on leaving, I passed your chair
and then spoke words
that tripped us,
into coming together.
And I push away
the thought
we might never have . . .

Can fear travel?
I'm only asking . . .
can fear travel backwards
and undo the moment when I passed your chair
and spoke the words . . .
that led us to
not just holding hands, but gripping hard,
stepping into an
uncertain future.

January 2013

# Frisson

There are things he does to me
that I have
waited for . . .
for half my life

made known to me
by touch
is the
length of my arm

from across the room
I see his hands
and
shivering . . .

remember.

July 2012

# Beached

Come down with me
and we will shift the sand
that lies beneath,
feel the grit,
be pricked by tiny pointed shells
ground by the waves
into bits
too small to bear a name.

Fog, press down and stifle wind
until the crest of cliff
with wildly waving sea-grass
is silent
stalk resting on stalk
rasping
only now and then . . .

Nothing so languorous as windless night
to raise an arm is only
to lose it in the hazy air,
and when we stretch our limbs
and roll to the water's edge
we swim among sea creatures
in a flurry of phosphorescence.

We are beached until morning
when fog lifts, wind rises
and a disappearing moon pulls the tide about,
hungry wavelets
rush up the flattened sand
erasing the shape of our nest and,
merciless,
even the footprints
that marked our coming.

February 2023

# Song of the Blood

You will never escape me,

the aroma of my skin
is in the air
you breathe

the texture of my hair
obscures the landscape
on which you gaze

and in your veins
blood surges,
seeking

the sound of my blood,
those two dark streams
come together,

separate
and come together
again,

weaving a net
from which
neither you nor I

wishes to escape.

January 2012

# The Taste of Sweetness

Consider acting the fool
staying awake past the eleventh hour
walking the length of the house
to hear laughter at midnight
and taste spice like sweetness
on your tongue.

Close your eyes to savor darkness
suspend yourself
on old knees made young
and at the edge of sweetness
let go and
sink into feathered sleep.

In the morning
slowly open your eyes
see the hands of time rest lightly
on a scandalous hour
and if, in a cerebral head,
the taste of sweetness lingers

then once again
consider playing the fool.

September 2012

# Twenty Times a Day

I think about your body
at least twenty times a day

you think I lie,
but flashes of memory

shamelessly rise up in my waking hours,
first stroke of a hand, first entry,

but most often, first drop
on to an arm, a chest,

the real breath-catcher being the scrape
of a leather watch-strap across my back.

My skin, no fool, lights up
already knowing what will come

in all its infinite variations.
Why not? my mind says,

staying cool,
in fleeting images,

Why not remember?

March 2012

# Poem for Next Tuesday

If I could turn the clock back
to the time of my return
I would be blond again
newly tanned
with a nubile body
white only from breasts to hips

And you would ravish me
before I had climbed
halfway up the stairs
not in the front hall
but the stairs outside
leading up to the front door

And we would not care
if all the world could see.

March 2013

# On Not Being Lysistrata

*You light up the room,*
may not only be said
to a beautiful woman.

In your maleness
there is no aura . . .
rose or otherwise,
forget such foolishness,
but at the sight of you

I feel my hand
on the bones of your ribs,
on the smooth skin of your thigh
I feel a thudding within me
like stones falling, and I know

I have lost my circadian rhythm
in the want of you
at noon
at two
at five in the afternoon.

March 2014

# The Reality of Flesh

*(Grotesquerie)*

I want to push away reality as we know it
and have three breasts or more
to bang about your ears,
feel beneath my ribs a place
where, at a touch,
I could be pierced straight through,
and beneath my eyes
you would find three mouths
one to tease
one to kiss
and one to bite.

You would grow another hand
and with it
pull out the length of your arms
to wrap twice around me,
but to tempt and thwart you
I would be covered
from head to toes
with Godiva's golden hair.

Do you not wonder that
when we play the game
following some rules
abandoning others
somehow we both win
even without such mad excess?

January 2014

# To My Surprise

In the half-dark of early morning
we meet in the hallway
you, fully dressed,
a foil to my intentions
but you lead me back to bed
and as a sign
of your intermittent kindness
take off your shoes
before climbing in to lie with me
where
embracing your woolly presence
I immediately fall asleep.

March 2014

# Through a Mist Darkly

We came at just the right time
to that Cornell hill
to watch the sun set
on a night
when there would be no sunset
and we would see
blanketing the valleys
a moving mist
that gave palpable measure
to the distance
between us and the farthest hills

We stood on that Cornell hill
the ground dropping away
beneath our feet
and when stars began to prick
the darkening sky
we saw an echo of lights
coming up through the mist
telling of little electric lives
in the city down below.

Another time we might come
to that Cornell hill
sit placidly on stones
and watch the sun, unclouded,
set over the city of Ithaca,
but for all its fiery glory
it would not stir us half as much
as the memory of an evening mist
moving among the hills
and the doubling below us
of a thousand winking stars.

July 2015

# On Fait de la Comédie

*Fakery and Sham*


He wears a façade of fine clothing,
a tailored shirt and tie
of good label,
to cover
the emptiness within.

He breaks faith with no one
since he is careful
to make no promises,
and his conversation is sprinkled
with, "I could care less . . ."

He puts forth a clever mind
to distract new friends
and skirts around deep feeling
as though it might burn
the giver,

But sham is an empty vessel
and he hopes in vain
that, for a time,
surface charm

will fool the world
and all the people in it.




October 2021

# SECTION VII: *CAPRICCIO*

## MILD HUMOR

Of Dregs and Legs
The Gates of Heaven
The Trouble with Venerable Maxims . . .

## Of Dregs and Legs

Jane, Jane, of tennis fame
has let the ball go down the drain.

Daphne S, pronounced Daphné,
no longer practices ballet.

Pool class and therapy are just the dregs
but promise cure for ailing legs.

So bring on the wine, both whites and reds,
let the coffee percolate,

there are things we still can do,
let's drink and eat and celebrate.

December 2016

# The Gates of Heaven

When I arrived
in my elderly Subaru
I was taken aback by the appearance
of those listing portals.
Though beautifully crafted
they looked worn and rusted and
I wondered whose hands
had once bent the iron
gilded the leaves.
Do angels do such heavy work,
or was it the lot of miscreants
who had to earn their place in heaven?

Magic on earth can be a fraud
an entertainment full of tricks,
in this unearthly place
could magic be real?
What a lovely surprise
to learn that angels simply
set their hands to any task—
and it is done,
no crowbar, blowtorch, bellows needed
no blistered palms of mortal blacksmiths.

Drawn by the air from
beyond those gates
I leave my car without regret
anxieties have fogged its windows
doubts lie bundled on the seat.
It's done its job
and brought me here,
now it's up to me to walk away
still unsure of what I'll find,

one small hope I carry with me—
whatever's on the other side
should match the life I left behind.

January 2022

# The Trouble with Venerable Maxims . . .

. . . is that they capture a corner of truth we have long been avoiding.
I am thinking of one, "Anything that can happen, probably will happen."
and have found that if you live long enough, it is a given.

A favorite story by James Thurber is "The Night the Bed Fell."
Read long ago, I do not remember exactly how the event came about,
but we were about to find out.

Well, for one thing, when the collapse comes, it is a great shock to the body
and spirit, but it also initiates a fountain of laughter. This is not a sober happening.

As we clambered out of downed bed slats, splintered side-rails and tumbled
duvets, we at least had the privilege, living in a big old house, of having five
other beds from which to choose.

The next day, having recovered my equanimity, it was up to me to call upon a
faithful handyman to assess the damage. He had previously come to solve
problems with warped doors and plugged pipes, but surveying the scene,
he declared the bed fixable and started off to fetch the right tools and
necessary new parts.

I thought he and I had carried off the encounter with admirable discretion, but
on leaving, he turned back for a moment, and said, "It's an old bed, Daphne.
Better go easy on the acrobatics."

April 2021

# SECTION VIII: *SONATA*

### CHILD AND SELF

Beginnings
Shoo, Shoo, Babies,
Memoir of a Five-Year-Old
In a New Place
Children's Rhymes
Some Kids Have It Easy . . .
My Hour at the Museum
Going to the Movies
Memories of New York, a Nickel's Worth
Ode to a Diamond Ring
Quién Era?
Other Rooms, Other Realities
A Beautiful Being
It Is Ignoble . . .
Idiots and Savants in the Labor Room
October Birthday
Continuity
Goodbye, Sweet Gallery
I Want the Sun to Burn Me
We Are So Small

# Beginnings

Born into a tropic clime,
out-doors to in, a golden time,
the molten sun each day bore down
on leaves from waxy green to brown
they seemed to bend beneath a weight
too hot to dwindle or abate
but hidden deep within the shade
the trees held flowers,
      petals splayed
to send forth heavy scent
in air, both thick and redolent
of color come alive
a silent buzz as from some hive
of bees that flew from bush to tree

so young, I thought it all for me.

January 2019

# Shoo, Shoo, Babies,

*(Back, Back, in Georgetown, Guyana)*

Sister, sister!
Listen to the jungle birds!
Whoop, whoop, whoop!
Their calls rise in the early morning air,
warm now, but later hot, hot,
killing damp,
killing hot.
We love all of it
sister, sister and I,
we do not know what cool is.

Nanny comes.
Shoo, shoo, she says,
under the house with you!
Now! she says . . .
our gawky house,
like all the others in Georgetown,
built on stilts, four corners,
east, west, north, south,
mahogany floor boards over our heads
to give us shelter from the sun.
Oh, Nanny, we know to obey,
we belong to you,
so under we go
to play in the shade.

But we are naughty babies,
Miss Norma, sister, sister, sticks out her head,
Miss Daphne, I, stick out my head
into the hot hot sun,
making laughter in our world.

It is our joy to tease Nanny Louisa
because we love her,
because we love her like a mother.

September 2018

# Memoir of a Five-Year-Old

*(Goodbye to Georgetown, British Guiana)*

Who knows what winds were blowing from the sea wall
        hard enough to change my life?

Who knows why cormorants sailed in the clouds above the ship
        then floated down to ride the spars and travel with me,
        but only so far, only so far

And who would listen in the night, to the screech of jungle birds
        whoop-whooping,
        so far, so very far away.

Did the name of the King of America matter, when the rain
        of soft blue jacaranda petals
        was lost in smoke-filled air?

The sea ran from cold to colder, but no one was watching,
        golden staterooms rang with laughter
        they seemed to know the all the answers,

The S.S. Maraval sailed on and on,
        leaning on the deck rail, I was too young to comprehend
        too young to cry.

May 2022

# In a New Place

My sister and I were born breathing the tropical air
        of Georgetown, Guyana
and later, the hot and cold extremes
        of New York.
In this teeming city, we were not alone in our foreignness
        but it took many years
        for us to feel American.

In school and on the streets,
we had some tough dealings with Irish kids
        who recognized and abhorred our British accents.
My sister put a stop to all that by grabbing some grapefruit halves
        out of a garbage can and squashing them
        all over the faces of our tormentors.
There is, it turns out, a certain respect for ingenuity
        among fighters.

In my adult life, among my friends . . .
        not admitting to enemies . . .
I am known as a 'tough lady'.
I do not relish the term, but I know where it comes from
        and do not hesitate to give full due to my forebears.
It was not, after all, the weak or the indecisive
        who landed on our shores
An inheritance of Slavic, German, English and British Colonial
        subsides into background
when I finally, and with pride, claim my identity
as an American.

April 2015

## Children's Rhymes

I am little, I am lost when I come to America
I see dark (our apartment), I feel cold (New York winter)
what I have brought with me is tropical heat and trees
flowering red, yellow and jacaranda blue.

*Birdie, birdie in the tree*
*sing a robin song to me.*

There were no robins in Guyana,
toucans and parrots, yes,
but I do not argue with English rhymes
and English stories

*Pease porridge hot, pease porridge cold*
*Pease porridge in the pot, five days old.*

My mother, new to the kitchen, cannot be accused
of bad cooking, but rice pudding and boiled potatoes
cannot appease a tongue longing for the bite
of our cook's Indian curry.

On the street, we are introduced to new rhymes,
"Appalling!" my father says,
from his seat on the couch
reading his paper.

*Rock, rock, rock the boat,*
*kill the captain, stay afloat,*
*Kill the sailor, 'spite his plea,*
*Throw them both in the deep blue sea,*

And to that fierce drumbeat, we run like hares
on cracked sidewalks
and jump from one foot to the other, ducking under two ropes
that rasp above our heads.

One day I am taken to church, and there overwhelmed
by the terrible darkness
I feel the air squeezed out of me
and quake with fear.

I cannot remember being afraid in Georgetown,
the nights were long and black, but the jungle is not silent,
it's alive with the coco-rico of frogs
and one nocturnal cry after another.

*Here is the church and here is the steeple*
*Open the doors and see all the people.*

Oh, yes!" I say, "Open the doors!" and rush out of the church
clutching my sister's hand, and when we reach our new home
I try not to be afraid of the shadowy hallways where shabby men
sometimes stand, whispering, "Come here, girlie!"

But out of the whorl of rhymes and games
light and heat
dark and cold
I am losing the old me, I can feel it.

I am gaining courage and street-smarts
which means learning to fight . . . or flee
and each day finds me ready . . . or almost ready
to play the next game, rhyme or no rhyme

that comes rolling down the alley.


January 2018

## Some Kids Have It Easy . . .

being American from the start, but I am going back
to the day I entered a NYC Public School
between Columbus and Amsterdam Avenue,
a stone building with a Gothic façade
which both impressed
and frightened me.

But I got over it,
I borrowed tough from my immigrant family
who had already made hard decisions to leave
everything they knew,
and board a ship
that would carry them to a new place
full of strangers.
who might turn out to be kind or cruel.

We were British, . . . and I know you will say,
"Oh, British!" . . . as though we were somehow different
from the Irish, the Germans and the Italians
who had made the journey before us.
But my sister and I met hostility
from Irish boys on the block
even before we entered school,
two girls with piping English accents.

There came a day in second grade where
I was truly mystified.
The teacher asked us to line up,
Americans on one side of the room,
'Foreigners' on the other,
and I went to join the foreigners . . .
at that time, Jewish refugees
who had escaped Nazi Germany.
But the clueless woman displayed her blatant prejudice
when she cried out,

"Oh, Daphne, whatever are you doing over there?"
and when I explained that I was 'foreign,'
born in British Guiana, she pulled me away, saying,
"No, my dear, you belong with the Americans."

Perhaps if I had been twelve I might have demurred,
done something! . . . it still gives me chills . . .
but I was seven, not fully formed in ideals or persona,
so I obeyed, and dared not ask for further explanation.
I was already living with the mystification
that a migrant child deals with every day.
Outside is America,
with all its warts and wonders,
home . . . with gradual estrangement . . .
is an old culture of food, friends and family.

Long after I left school,
through many and diverse circumstances,
my foreignness got whittled away,
but it's the kids who have it easy
who do not know
that it requires diligence and luck
to affect a balance and take on
a different skin.
In time, I finally assumed the privilege
of, not just saying, but feeling
that, I was, indeed, an American

January 2023

# My Hour at the Museum

(1936 A.D.)

I've been sent to this New York temple
where sculptures, busts and paintings
are meant to be admired.

I'm just a little girl from school
to be pushed and tutored and
have my imagination fired,

but I drift out to the garden where
the Hanuman Monkey God sits
in stony contemplation

and I cozy up to him
in his wicked funny world
and feel a strong temptation

to kick the leaf piles, run like a jungle cat
and leave behind the heavy art
of gilt and oil and stone

I just want to see my mother
who waits for me at home.

May 2021

# Going to the Movies

Taking a child to his first movie
is perhaps a banal part
of parenting
with a shared experience of
rabbits and piglets running
away from Sly Fox,
or Green Monster being
bested by a Hero
with a flat-drawn pretty face
and a highly-muscled body . . .

*If he flies all the time, mom,*
*why is he wearing shoes? . . .*

But the banal became bizarre
in the hands of my mother
whose choice of first movie for me to see
was 'The Bride of Frankenstein'.

A little coil of horror formed
behind my eyes
ineradicable even when we stepped out
into daylight
and what lay in store was my mother
deciding to shop, sending me up
to the apartment alone . . .

*Now that I'm six, I can have a key . . .*

where the sun coming through
the windows did not warm me
and in those empty rooms

for the first time
I knew what it meant
to be palpitatingly afraid.

July 2013

# Memories of New York, a Nickel's Worth

My life of crime started very early,
it had a lot to do with being a child
in the Depression Years
when having to spend a nickel
often seemed an insurmountable obstacle.

I was given fifty cents a week as carfare
to get to a school, not in our district,
but one of the best in the city,
so there was a tacit agreement with my mother—
who had spent a good deal of her young life living by her wits,
that if I could creep under the subway turnstile
when the man in the ticket booth wasn't looking
it was a nickel saved.

Tied into the corner of my handkerchief
were my two nickels' subway fare
but by the end of one terrible school day
one of those coins had slipped out
and since seven-year-olds are not
entirely hardened beings
I sat down on the curbstone and cried.
A policeman came over
and discovering the cause of my distress
gave me a nickel to go home.

I remember that I was not only thankful
but utterly astonished that anyone—
even a grown-up—
could so easily part with five cents.
I am not exaggerating when I say that
in my child's mind
it seemed like a miracle
but more than that

it burdened me
and I determined it had to be given back.

Days later, after a successful turnstile-creep
I attempted to return a nickel to the policeman
on our school crossing
only it turned out to be a different policeman
who tried and tried to refuse
but could see by my almost frantic insistence
he must take the coin from my grubby little hand
and, to my great relief,
finally accepted it.

In the way of children
we never questioned the motivations
of our resourceful mother.
Now we know she was an immigrant parent—
in this case British
but in essence no different
from the Germans, the Italians or the Irish—
who wanted for her children,
over any obstacle,
everything of the best
that America had to offer.

June 2010

# Ode to a Diamond Ring

I have brought into this room
a diamond ring.

It lives silently on my finger
but cannot quell
shooting rays of color
that dazzle walls and floors
and dance on eyes and ceilings.

As it tries to contain itself
in quiet faceted planes,
why does this cold stone
burn my hand . . .
as it burned her hand?

I wear my mother's diamond ring
and watch it shine brilliantly
but not kindly,
emitting a low keening sound
for those who wear it,
a cruel sparkler . . .

like my mother.

June 2016

# Quién Era?

*(Who was it?)*

Ayyyyy! Little girl!
why were you made to stand in the corner?

Who was it?

Your mother, angry at something you have done?
Your teacher, frustrated by the schoolwork
      you have not done?

You look rebellious when you should look humble,
your head is inclined downward
but your eyes are furious and have no tears.

I was that little girl
and years later
I prefer to walk in open spaces
I avoid corners
and admit that I am still afraid
of that hard, fixed angle
where two walls come together.

But we live always in sight of four walls,
whether close or far away,
they set our limits
and at times
they menace us.

Here I am, on my knees in the garden
pulling out weeds,
the flower beds enclosed by a stone wall,
so well-made, so beautiful
but in every crevice

I see a pair of eyes
very small and very brilliant
that belong to the serpents
who live in the wall

and, I know, that
all the time,
they are watching me
they are watching me.

August 2020

## Other Rooms, Other Realities

Our family, newly established in New York,
had brought with them, British rules and
    regulations, afternoon tea and bread pudding.
My father ate lamb chops for breakfast
    and with a touch of Victorian reserve,
    seldom spoke to his children.
My mother learned to cook Indian curry
    to satisfy our Guayana tastes,
but she already had gifted hands for knitting, sewing,
    embroidery, and, to fill out the picture,
    a very sharp tongue.

I assumed in those early years, as the young often do,
    that all households were exactly like ours,
until my sister and I went to school, where the hint
    of differences was often displayed.
But real revelations came from being invited after hours
    to the homes of our friends, and we glimpsed
    other worlds, diverse and fascinating,
our entry into America.

There were Irish friends whose homes seemed to us
    to be chaotic, stew bubbling on the stove
    raisiny soda bread on the table,
and a father who, after work, spent many hours
    at his favorite bar, and when he did appear,
    smelled of whiskey and false bonhomie,
trying to placate a wife, who, for good reason,
    was known as a scold.

I had, but could not admit envy, for the luxuries
    of a little rich girl,
whose father, seldom seen, owned a radio corporation,
    and whose mother never entered the kitchen.

Their skyscraper penthouse with a view of Central Park
      could not hide a certain kind of loneliness,
the long absences of those parents
      or the older sister always crying in her bedroom.

There was richness of another kind laid out before us,
      when the door opened on the homes of Jewish friends,
      refugees from Nazi Germany.
More than one of them had a father who played the violin,
      there was always a piano,
and walls filled with books, more books
      and bound music scores . . .

My reality was being roughed up and inevitably changed.
I could only speculate on the doors I might open
      in the now, and in the future,
by my new American self.

January 2020

# A Beautiful Being

I saw Mr. Klempner every week, fall, winter and spring. He was my piano teacher, young and mild-mannered. Even as a child, I was aware that the world drifted past him, as though he was in a cocoon. Except for his music, which was air and light and blood in his veins.

Among a bevy of piano students, I worked hard and memorized easily. I shirked many things in my young life, but never the sonatas we were working on.

At the end of the year, Mr. Klempner would sit at the piano and produce a concert for us. His playing was more than inspired, lifting us off the ground, as we sat in metal folding chairs on a faded oriental carpet, no other furniture in the room but two Steinway grand pianos.

My lessons ended abruptly, when he enlisted in the army in World War II. Much later, he told me that, discerned as useless, they had assigned him to be an organist for a very ardent chaplain, who kept adding services to the usual Sunday ritual. The chaplain made the mistake of asking Myron what he would think of fitting in yet another service, and Myron's reply was, "Why, Sir, don't you try giving just one good one, instead?"

He was transferred immediately, which is what the army does, and to my endless gratitude, he survived the war.

I went to visit him when I was sixteen, leaving for college, and he told me I should continue practicing and not regret my absence from him. He reminded me that certain difficult passages in the pieces I was studying had solved themselves over my untutored summers.

"You will see." he said, with his shy smile.

Advice, so low-key, so thoughtful, both true and inexplicable, but it led me to realize how unreservedly I loved Mr. Klempner, an embodiment of music and unworldliness.

August 2019

# It Is Ignoble . . .

to want always to be the best in the class
        in the gym
        at the ballet barre
        taking an exam.
The teachers in school encouraged me
        to a fault
when they should have come down on me hard,
        kind or unkind.

But there was reckoning in the dance studio
where the ballet mistress was
        cool, harsh and Russian.
She had no praise for my shallow brilliance
        and I learned that words,
        unsought and unexpected,
can change the trajectory of your life.

I fell out of childish love with myself
when Tatiana Asimova took me by the shoulder,
        turned me away from the mirror,
        and said,
"Vot you tink you are, Duffeny,
        Kewpie Doll?"

May 2011

# Idiots and Savants in the Labor Room

I've lived long enough to know
it's a pain like no other.
It fashions a cocoon,
eliminating all other senses
yet leaves you rational—if afloat—
at discreet intervals.

Novelists (male authors), even good ones,
describe a crescendo of pain and screams
from behind a closed door . . .
which seems nonsense to me.
The sounds that you hear are deep groans
such as a labourer might make
while pulling a cart full of stones.

Frequently left to yourself, it seems that
the people, when they do surround you, are idiots,
understanding nothing of what is going on
while you deal with inevitability and the miraculous.

With my second child since I knew what I was about,
I was so quiet that, while the savants were out in the hall,
smoking, and waiting for something to happen,
I was left with a young student nurse
who, in some distress, kept crying out,
"Oh, please don't, Mrs. Solá!"
My somewhat crabby response was,
"Oh, shut up, and catch the baby."

At a later time, modernity had entered the hospital
and they fixed up mirrors so I could watch the birth,
but at the edge of pain was euphoria,
I could not hear, I could not see
and I felt an unuttered scream rising up in me

because I had entered that room
as one
and would leave it
as two.

June 2011

# October Birthday

You have to see a boy standing up to his waist
in a pile of leaves
he is five
and with time holding still
as it does at that age
he will be five five more times
on his birthday
and then six three times
but he will be seven just once
because now he is in school
where they teach about time
that is what schools do,
*Where are the hands on the clock, Matthew?*

Still the day comes when he is seven
and his shrieks of joy are augmented
by five young friends
who jump out of the cars their mothers are driving
and run up the hill
always little legs running, running,
because the piles of leaves so carefully raked
by a young father
are waiting to be demolished
to be jumped on, scattered and kicked
while the grown-ups on the porch
fiddle about with lemonade and paper cups
talking and barely noticing.

But years later
they will remember the innocent mayhem
and how time held still
for the boy standing up to his waist
in a pile of chestnut leaves
who was five five times
was six three times

but seven
heartrendingly
only once.

October 2015

# Continuity

It's a lost day when I do not think of my father's hands,
always, with assurance, able to do things,
      make things,
      take things apart
      and put them back together.
He once told me that his exam to become a licensed
      watchmaker was to take apart a watch
      down to its miniscule parts,
then re-assemble them into working order,
      all in a given time.

In a world where sprockets and wheels have been
      replaced by codes and algorithms
I long for the tactile and the real, which allowed
      my father to make miniature eyeglasses
      for our dolls
and join with my mother to squeeze apricots and plums
      into a bathtub, where
      with some alchemy,
they produced homemade gin
      during Prohibition years.

You have to believe that, from my father, I inherited
      my right hand,
      strong, stubby, infinitely adept
      at nailing, sanding, and planting things,
while from my mother comes a left hand,
      fingers and nails attenuated and elegant
yet capable of holding pieces of cloth
      or wool and knitting needles
from which we fashioned dresses, curtains,
      scarves, sweaters,
and I remember this as far more rewarding than
      the shop-shop-shopping, in which
      we are now pressed to indulge.

At this late date, I can be satisfied by blessed continuity,
    when I see my children, each in their own way,
incorporating tactile arts into their
    modern techno-driven lives.

May 2011

# Goodbye, Sweet Gallery

I would expect Memory to be long
and stretch over thirty years
like an elastic band
easily gathering Art and Things
into an indiscriminate bundle.

But Memory is capricious.
In my art gallery,
Picasso loomed large,
but Matisse was more luminous than the golden bracelets,
and Utamaro had no need to seek the light
he *is* the light, that shines equally
on a single bijin, a young woman seated by a laundry tub
or a passel of beauties at the edge of the sea.

The three of them barely made room for Hokusai
who could draw anything standing on his head
and did so with abandon for eighty-five years . . .
assuming he did not take up pen or brush
until he was four.
And they paid no attention to Miró,
a giggler and a dazzler
with his bursts of color and loopy black lines
who yet manages to lift being funny into a higher realm.

Sometimes Memory plays at theater
giving Art and Things each, their chance
in the spotlight.
But for me, looking back has lost its luster
and I beg Memory to do no more.
My elasticity is growing brittle around the edges.

What I have left, what I hold with two hands
pressed hard against me
is the Present
short on glory or significance,
satisfied by only casual meetings
with great Art and Music,
but I am pleased by a succession of forgotten moments,
by an hour of unexpected pleasure
and a run of completely un-noted,
un-notable days.

September 2015

# I Want the Sun to Burn Me

I want the sun to burn me
flood my skin with color
and turn the hair on my arms to gold

But, in so doing, the sun may not harm me.

I want water to flow over me
pull me down
wrap seaweed around my feet

and untangle my hair
until it floats out
behind me

But water may not drown me.

Some few will have known me
my grace
and my clumsiness

my unquenchable thirst
for ephemerals
that tantalize

keeping themselves just out of reach.

Some few still hear my voice
turn their heads
to grasp at all that is left

of the nymph become flower,

inescapable memory.

January 2023

# We Are So Small

When morning breaks
the trees stand silent
each one a black presence
fracturing the sky into lozenges of light
but it does not take long for them
to gather force and pride
in their own majesty,
march down the hill
to the shore of the lake,
spurn dropping into its leaden depths
and cross it
like Jesus Christ in full command.

Nothing can stop them
as they march up the hill
on the other side
and make their way
across a continent.

No match for their life span,
at their feet
we come and go,
come and go . . .
we are so small,
busy, possessed,
a spectrum of piccolo voices .

Perhaps in the highest branches,
allowance must be made for larger souls,
Mozart trilling birdsong
Sappho and Virgil weaving poetic lines
among the leaves,
and on basest ground,

Stalin growling like a bear
as he carves hearts and livers
into a roughened trunk,
echoes and vibrations,
these and more should last forever.

But when dusk approaches
the fading light barely illuminates
our darting figures.
Overtaken by night,
we are so small,
so very small.
O, see us bestriding fallen branches,
bearing tiny burdens
as we come and go . . .
                 and go.

July 2021

# About the Author

Daphne Solá lives in Jacksonville. NY in a country setting. She is a pianist, a printmaker, and the owner of an art gallery. Solá studied bookmaking at Wells College Summer Book Arts Institute and produces artist-books as well as chapbooks combining her poems and art, including *Perry City Poems* (2022). Solá and her husband spent many years in Peru, as is reflected in her work and art which has exhibited in New York, Lima, Peru, Copenhagen, Denmark, and Nara, Japan. Her work includes silkscreens, embossed prints, artist-made paper, and hand-printed poetry books.

Her poems have been published in *The Healing Muse, From the Finger Lakes: A Poetry Anthology, From the Finger Lakes: A Memoir Anthology, Onager Editions, Prime of the Ithaca Times,* and *Bluff & Vine*. Solá has visited Japan many times and in 1983 attended a Papermakers Conference in Kyoto, which reflected her continuing love of paper in all forms. When asked about the moves from one art form to another, she says, "It's really all the same thing."

www.ingramcontent.com/pod-product-compliance
Lightning Source LLC
Chambersburg PA
CBHW072143160426
43197CB00012B/2220